In 1995, I opened an African American bookstore in Richardson, TX. Once a month, a Poetry & Prose night was put on for the local young artist to come out and read their writings and their thoughts, their hearts... their insights. Anthony Walker would have been a featured poet on any given night, only if he had written his book 25 years earlier.

I received a copy of the book at a time when issues of voter registration and police shootings were paramount. Yet, when I read it, I found it to be uplifting. I also suffered a devastating loss as a result of the COVID-19 pandemic and I struggled for a long time with my grief. On a sleepless night I picked up "My Father's Dreams" to help with the restlessness. I read "The Love Of My Life, Gone". And then it happened... tears were rolling down my cheeks and I could not contain myself. These words touched the deepest part of my soul. Each line voiced feelings I had inside me, feelings of hurt and sadness over my loss that I was unable to release. Anthony's words were my antidote. How could he know that his words would play such an intricate role in my healing?

Anthony works somewhere between the spiritual and social consciousness, yet he emulates the prose of the iconic Black poets of the Harlem Renaissance.

Review by Kenneth Davis

# MY FATHER'S DREAMS

*A Collection of Poetic Prose*

Anthony Walker

My Father's Dreams
Copyright © 2021 by Anthony Walker

All rights reserved. No part of this publication may be reproduced, distributed, or transmitted in any form or by any means, including photocopying, recording, or other electronic or mechanical methods, without the prior written permission of the author, except in the case of brief quotations embodied in critical reviews and certain other non-commercial uses permitted by copyright law.

ISBN
978-1-954932-59-3 (Hardcover)
978-1-954932-66-1 (Paperback)
978-1-954932-65-4 (eBook)

*In honor of Jupiter Hammon, the first black poet to be published. He was born a slave and died a slave, but his gift didn't die when he went to the grave. It lives on in the lives of writers like myself, who understand the power of prose!*

# Table of Contents

My Word ................................................................. 1

Sunday Mornings .................................................. 3

Now You Be the Judge ....................................... 5

In My Garden ....................................................... 7

Just a Vision .......................................................... 9

Soul of an Artist ................................................. 11

Emotion for the Black Child ........................... 13

Mumbo Jumbo .................................................. 15

The Inspiration to Praise ................................. 17

Speaking Success into the Wind .................... 19

The Love of My Life, Gone! ............................ 21

For the Love of the Family .............................. 23

Oh, Yes, We Can! (Ode to Obama) ................ 25

Underground Man ............................................ 27

When She Cries (Teenage Slave) .................... 29

When the Page Turns ....................................... 31

What Have I Got to Prove? ............................. 33

Prison Calm ........................................................ 35

I Do It for My Mama ........................................ 37

Patience and Understanding ........................... 39

| | |
|---|---|
| Especially 4 U | 41 |
| All God's Children | 43 |
| Unjust Us | 45 |
| Quit Bringing up My Past | 47 |
| I Believe | 49 |
| The Real G Has Spoken | 51 |
| Streets of Sorrow | 53 |
| Beautiful People | 55 |
| She Loves Me 'Cause… | 57 |
| The Canvas of Creation | 59 |
| Black Romeo | 61 |
| The Gift and the Giver | 63 |
| The Psalmist | 65 |

# My Word

Poetry is an art. It's music from the heart, the essence of words, the beauty of thoughts. Never thought I could shout to be so eloquent and command verbal excellence in a manner so pleasant. But don't mistake my character as one who's a farce. I'm the harbinger of misfortune from the dungeon of man's faults. To arise, I've risen to channel peaks of wisdom, defined my visions and the dreams that come with them. It's my time now to give and not take, so I've evolved as a writer from an ominous place. A poet who didn't know it, I kept my mouth shut and thought in the dark about how to write best. It's a peaceful pleasure extended as a treasure when my melody exudes from the pen. A wistful collection—my word, my expression.

# Sunday Mornings

The melody of a blue jay chirping into the air sets the tone for another beautiful morning. As I roll back the covers, I smile at the thought of nature introducing me to the dawn of a new day. When my feet hit the floor, I'm prompted to groom as the aroma of sausage, biscuits, and eggs pervades my senses. Staring into the mirror at my disheveled features, a thought strikes me, a startling revelation. It's Sunday morning! Mother has extended the invitation and all but demanded my presence at the worship service. As always, I'm lethargic at the idea of attending another pretentious fashion show where the patrons arrive in their best holy rags. I've made my decision, and on it I'll stand, so I make my way into the kitchen alcove to greet my wife with a kiss. She understands. As we face each other at the breakfast table, the conversation centers on family. Pausing as the silence of the moment sets in, we sip from our coffee mugs and squint our eyes as the warm vapors rise. There's no need for any more idle chatter, so we scurry off to our favorite place, the sundeck. So here we are her, me, and the wailing sax of Kenny G. It doesn't get any better than this, a moment of pure bliss. It's Sunday, the one day we've set aside to relish the morning, side by side.

# Now You Be the Judge

An eye for an eye and a tooth for a tooth was once the fairest measure of judgment among men. When one wrongs a society with one's deviant behavior, the cause is never considered to determine why. Should a poor man steal to feed his family when the security of a job has vanished like a magic carpet? In the state of an economy maliciously inequitable, should the rich hold on and continue to hoard their wealth? Can one ever be right if they've done things wrong even though amends have been made at the foot of God's throne? Our manner of dress, the way we speak, and even the complexity of our racial heritage force us into the narrow corridors of caste and class. So we strive for the pinnacle of social excellence only to look down on our fellow man. A towering height of prejudiced concerns has accomplished nothing but war between the nations! "God Bless America" was the anthem of the forefathers that carried with it great promise and optimistic ideals. It was issues such as same-sex unions and the sacrifice of human life that brought down the wrath of judgment on Sodom and Gomorrah. I wonder whether man's demise would be the same if such vile and wretched evils should plague us again.

# In My Garden

In my garden, I've sown seeds of righteousness to reap a harvest of peace and happiness. But before I could plant anything with my hands, I first had to till and cultivate my land. When the ground became fertile and ready to receive, I scattered love as the primary seed. In the very next patch, I sprinkled some virtue, a great attribute for love to grow close to. I wanted an increase in the knowledge of God's will, so I planted the Word for the roots to fulfill. Maintained my labor, uprooting weeds of worry, anticipating my return but not in a hurry. The rain will come to give birth to my seeds and nurture the earth to replenish man's need. It also tempers the wilted souls so the sun can cause their leaves to unfold. Now when my harvest comes in bountiful measures as plentiful as the need, I'll gather my fruit a blessing indeed and express my gratitude on bended knees.

# Just a Vision

I was thinking but not out loud with emotion or subjectivity. In my mind, I traveled at a pace that led me to a place if it could be imagined; I considered heaven. In my mind's eye, there was a glare from up there, so brilliant, engulfing me from head to toe, almost too exuberant to behold, yet I remained focused. And yes, I was in awe! I'll tell you what I saw: the glory of God was an amazing sight that permeated everything, and the sphere of his gaze was fascinating as it pierced right through me. The gardens were green, the rivers crystal clear, and everyone sang with a loud voice to hear. There was praise upon praise heaped upon praise. No discord or reason for alarm; even the wildest of beasts were embraced with charm. I can't go on. You'll think I'm exaggerating or assume that I believe what I saw and that it's not beyond me, and maybe someday I'll be whisked away.

## Soul of an Artist

When the heart grows cold from a fondness for pleasure, only you know the relentless drive that fuels your soul. Contemplating the challenges that make you so bold, basking in solitude as your life unfolds. As each day paces, you strive and toll, thrusting your way upon the world to leave a legacy untold, not to receive accolades from some prestigious bunch. That's not why an artist bares his soul. It has much to do with what God placed inside you to reach a plateau so others see it too. Never feeling whole unless you give it your all, the mark is for excellence although sometimes you fall. But one is not merely an artist, and one is not merely judged as an artist. For the arts have a purpose—action!

# Emotion for the Black Child

An image of reality captured in the eyes of the hopeful as they peer into life's kaleidoscope, uncertain of the road ahead. Blessed to be here, brazen, beyond fear, until the demons of history stumble onto their pathway. Then the black child can see that he's regarded as an enemy and a beast of burden in the land of a vicious clan. Won't the preachers take a stand to address our seed as they proceed into the streets as Crips, Bloods, hustlers, and thieves? Though their hearts become callous and desperately wicked, we can't ignore them now. Can't vilify their stance. It's no surprise. There's a void in our heritage—the dark side. Without knowledge and customs of our ancestral tribes, the concept of community has all but died. So who's to blame for this merciless game of thug life passion for ghetto fame? Enough of this rhetoric about black-on-black crime and the squandering of the dream of Dr. Martin Luther King. Tupac didn't die in vain; he knew his name would live on. He was the epitome of our struggle both right and wrong. The voice of rap music is the modern-day *griot*, warning us of a present state of mind. If you listen well, you may hear them tell the agony of being left behind. Emotions unwind when we look upon their faces and see our reflection in subtle traces. Now the man in the mirror has to look deeper. The black child is not a problem. He's lacking a teacher!

# Mumbo Jumbo

No poem can be said where reason has fled, so allow me to spiel these thoughts from my head. Upon my deathbed, spiked with needles of hatred, I'm so confused as to the superlative of a patriot. This is my country, 'tis, o thee bloodstained land of liberty. So who will hear this ritual of fear, borne out of decimation and cultural annihilation? Eastward bound, where the sun does rise and the juju man flutters and jabs at the skies, I turn my face and make prayers to erase the disgusting and despicable hatred of my race. I'm in black skin. Did my ancestors sin and turn the tables of fate? This rabble-rouser of spirit and poet of determination has determined to startle the elitist of this nation. So fix your mind beyond modern times, and compare your plight to that of mine. Imprisoned for a crime beyond my will, my mind still soars while my body is still. This conflict of inertia is a power within itself that urges me to speak above poverty, beyond wealth.

# The Inspiration to Praise

As I kneel in God's presence before the throne of grace and mercy, there's a feeling beyond words that always seems to move me. Even standing in the congregation with my hands lifted high, no earthly distractions to obscure my focus. Thinking of Him as I'm walking down the block, an emotion erupts from the pit of my soul. When I'm faced with a dilemma and burdened by crisis, I lift mine eyes to the holy hill of Zion and cry out. Overwhelmed with thoughts of anxiety, enticed by what the world has to offer, that's when I'm in the heat of battle and thankful for His armor. It has been decreed that everything breathing should offer up the sacrifice of praise. How can I deny that He's worthy of such adoration when He's been so good to me! A testament of lovingkindness led me to repent. The comfort of the Holy Spirit has made my heart content. Each day, I express my thankfulness as a token of appreciation. Now that he's repaired the breach of separation, He longs to be the God of this nation.

# Speaking Success into the Wind

God breathed on me again a message of hope to inspire my dreams and give new ambition to the purest desires that have formed within me. From a dark mood inhibiting crater of society, a passion has been awakened in me to live and not die in vain! So I speak positive affirmations after hearing the Master's voice urging me to be forward minded, come what may. One day at a time, I'm determined to reach my destiny while striving for excellence to live upright, at the height of my potential, to love in this cruel world. I remember from whence I came, the struggles, the pain. It was all a part of the plan. But now that I see far beyond me, no more cowering from my commitment to humanity. If no one else will speak success into my ears, I'm motivated to tell myself that I have a right to the tree of life, and it's quite all right if I aspire for greatness. It's my life. I'll just have to live it.

# The Love of My Life, Gone!

There she goes again. I see her in my dreams, and with every waking moment, she passes through the corridors of my mind, as if she's insistent on torturing me for a love once lost. Gone! How can I move on when the brevity of life can't be calculated? It's tough at times, but just maybe there's hope that I can recover the fragments of my heart that were torn away. Gone! Yes, she's to blame, the reason why I play the game of holding out hoping within for a chance encounter with the lady in my dreams again. Cause she's gone! I was wrong, I know. I take blame for refusing to acknowledge and enhance her beauty, to allow her pedals to shed so she might bloom as radiant as a rose. So she's gone! And now I want her back to face destiny with me, to make me whole, to set me free. But she's gone.

# For the Love of the Family

The tree of life extends from one generation to the next when a child is born out of a passionate storm onto the stage of misfortune. His people have been mistreated, miseducated, and methodically displaced—a reversal of roles among the human race. A mother and father with but one thing to do, shun the rigorous routine of social bondage to nurture the child with the oral tradition that was whispered into their ears. The other siblings have mastered the art of walking in love. Even when their feet are bare, strength comes from above. It was thought that to divide would certainly conquer them, but Mother embodied the spirit of survival and would not let the branches die off. Now that we're wiser and much, much stronger, we're no longer ignorant but glean from the past. The family must live on and testify to the world that God's love is sufficient and greater than any peril.

# Oh, Yes, We Can! (Ode to Obama)

We can eliminate words like "lynching" and "profiling," for they were the products of a time when ill-conceived thought was pervasive, assuming one life should be valued over another. Yes, I was inspired the first time I heard the commanding voice of Martin Luther King as he revealed a dream that was so obviously inspired by God. Yes, we can! The concept is vibrant, spirited, and holistic in nature and serves as an anthem to revive the nation. Although the presence of evil abides in the status quo, a remnant will rise to stem the tide. I'm optimistic because I know we can, and we will, transform our world into a better place. Some values need restoring. Others need to be replaced. If we look deep within ourselves to question our integrity, morality comes into play. Are we willing to be free and allow others to be, as blessed as God has fashioned them to be? The time has come and gone. It's written in stone that Obama's legacy will forever live on. There are mountains to peak and valleys to climb that will mark this historic time. And those who succeed us will be proud to read the accomplishments of this iconic figure in light of our journey from slavery to today. Yes, we can!

# Underground Man

On higher ground, the stage is set for the vilest of men to achieve their best. Those whom we esteem exploit the masses as they spill champagne from their crystal glasses. No sweat off their noses. It's spite in our face, expenses of waste, a tasteless disgrace. The aspirant of dreams that never materialize has blood in his eyes and refuses a disguise. Forced into the gutter beneath the streets to cavort with others, burdened by defeat. The claim to fame has altered his quest for personal, social, and financial success. But he hasn't given up. No, not yet. He's still a man despite his regrets. The sewer system is intricate. He's learned to master it while ignoring the rodents that gnaw at his confidence. The crabs in this bucket are all the same. They've resigned not to reach the top. So when one falls in with the urge to win, they claw him on the spot. But that tunnel of light that's brightest at night is a beacon for the underground man. He may never rise again. That's quite all right, but in his heart, he'll continue to fight. Clamoring, uncensored at his insidious plight, society can't hear. They've cast him out of sight.

# When She Cries
## (Teenage Slave)

The sadness in her eyes, the pain she can't hide, spills her emotions at times. Her world is so fragile, yet fear is no factor. She doesn't even grieve about what she sees. Involuntary tears will never tell the horrors of her story, the living hell. Forced into womanhood at the age of twelve, love and affection were things she never felt. She accepted the fact that her mother had sold her. No one cared, so no one told her that she probably wouldn't live to see twenty-one. Her fate as a prostitute was sealed and done. Just how much can a young girl take before the jagged edges of her heart wilt and break? Many times, it's crossed her mind to end it all with honor, but that would be the coward's way, so she dries her eyes to face another day. When her tears do fall, it's only an effort to suppress the thoughts of her adolescence. Now that her life has taken a turn, a deadly virus contracted, no one's concerned. But on her deathbed, she finds the strength to write a short story of how her life came and went. Her tear-stained pages sound an alarm for those among us who see no harm in exploiting young girls for pleasure or gain. Would it make a difference if we could feel her pain?

# When the Page Turns

A whisper of the wind may echo to a child that life is like a canvas that awaits the abstract. With the stroke of imagination and the genius of wit, young minds flourish where love exists. But evolution has its place in the heartbeat of the human race, subtly erasing innocence and faith. Teenage years are now clouded with fears of a culture of retribution. Oh, what a price to pay! A whisper of the wind may echo to a man that life is an adventure only conquered by the risqué. Tolerance of the abnormal is the mystique of masculinity. It's the elephant in the room men choose not to see. But one day, he'll awaken and regretfully say, "I have truly lost my way." Oh, what a price to pay! A whisper of the wind may echo to a friend that life will one day reward honesty, integrity, and accountability. She may say to the great, "You are not so wise, even though you shine in the light of public eyes." This narrative being written will tell the tale of an era of technology unparalleled. But the winds of change are swirling above, waiting to descend on the wings of a dove.

# What Have I Got to Prove?

Like the palm tree that bends in the wind, I've withstood the turbulent storms of heartache and strife. Much of my existence and experience in life has led to internal conflict with no resolution in sight. A fighter by nature, I've learned to contend with my greatest opponent, the in-a-me within. So why avert my attention from this noble quest that challenges me to rise, or why compromise the truth I've learned for a false sense of acceptance? I have no bones to pick with others concerning their worldview. I'm much too busy listening for the voice to argue just to prove a point. I didn't ask for the struggle, suffering, or pain, but without it, I've learned there's not much gained. To understand this concept is to know humility and accept the person you are destined to be.

# Prison Calm

The smooth, hard face trained to indicate nothing to a prison guard, neither slavishness nor resistance. Bound by a code of ethics to see no evil, hear no evil, speak no evil. Muted by circumstances without companion or recourse at hand. When men of certain creeds are compelled by their need to continue their lives as brawlers and thieves, fighting and hustling becomes the order of the day, yet one finds time to slip away and pray, meditating in the midst of the storm, with nerves of steel, embracing faith to determine God's will. To the left men fall, defeated by the letters of the alphabet *(A, I, D, S)*. Meanwhile, others become despondent, and their souls find no rest. The prison doctor seems vexed and somewhat perplexed by the tranquil serenity this one man possessed. He treads against the grain unscathed, sane, social etiquette intact despite the *X* on his back. His energy is rare, harnessed to the peak of perfection. His diction refined, versatile, and selective. Conditioned to smile while beaming on the inside, cool, calm, collected, taking one day at a time.

# I Do It for My Mama

She believed in me when no one else would and cleaned up my mess when no one else could. The highest pedestal is reserved for her. The raging seas I'd quell for her. If I could offer my life to make things right, Mama would have it all. The things that make for an ordinary life are what she'd enjoy the most. I could hand her the moon and offer her the stars, but she'd be too humble to boast. So my dedication at best is to pass life's tests and make my mama proud. No longer will I rest or waste another day until I say, through my work, "I love you, Faye." In loving memory of a mother who can never be replaced.

# Patience and Understanding

The stairway to heaven is no easy road; there are trials along the way and misfortunes untold. But there is living proof that peace can be attained; it's evident upon the countenance of the least among men. Arrested development exacts a toll that envelopes the spirit and tarnishes the soul. There's no way to avoid heartache and pain; we simply need patience to understand such things. Some things are inevitable as time will reveal; so a man's conduct is his greatest appeal. The joy in understanding the beauty of our struggle is to know that we'll prevail. When the virtue of our character is weighed in the balance, our lives become a story to tell.

# Especially 4 U

While meditating on my thoughts—pondering, reasoning, lulling through a moment of insouciant peace—along comes your image to send my mind reeling and ignite a spark in my heart. The controversy is simple. I'm here and you're there, connected by a fleeting thought. I guess that's the core to the art of love, knowing that it hails from up above. Good times or bad, it shouldn't matter much, as long as our hearts can touch. It's always challenging when I'm separated from you. At times I'm really crushed. But I've learned to live inside my thoughts, to compensate for the time we've lost.

# All God's Children

Some of God's children have no shoes on their feet, and their bellies are swollen so they scavenge to eat. Some of God's children make their bed in the street in the villages of Nigeria— no rest, no relief. Some of God's children have no concept of abuse; their pain is so real, they're detached and aloof. Some of God's children grow bitter with age and curse the elders for their sinful ways. Some of God's children don't have the will to resist the urge to do whatever they feel. Some of God's children ain't got no blues, silver-spoon fed and angling for the moon. Some of God's children don't know how to give; they're greedy, presumptuous, and quick to steal. Some of God's children will bless you with a smile or a heartfelt greeting that lasts for a while. Some of God's children understand need; they even pray for rain to cultivate the seed. But all God's children are one and the same; we can shirk responsibility and misplace blame. But we're all God's children.

# Unjust Us

Time and again it happens, and the headlines read, "Another Black Teen Gunned Down in the Streets." But it's no longer the hooded mob; they've been silenced by fear and aggression. Nor was it the cops who fired the fatal shots. The irony of this tragedy lies in the fact that a life was devalued by another man who's black. Both selling crack seven days a week, climbing the addict's back to make ends meet. A feud erupted over land neither owned. A turf war ensued, and the weapons were drawn. At first, it was only a prideful standoff, until the innocent bystanders hurrahed for an onslaught. Just another typical day in the hood, where people don't intervene even when they could. So there's no need to wail and march for justice when the wounds of culture are inflicted by us!

# Quit Bringing up My Past

I'm often reminded of the man I used to be—the women I confused, the people I used, the crimes I committed for personal gain, how I hurt my family, the suffering, the pain. But I don't have to listen to that voice telling me that I'm just no good and I'll never be. I've finally learned to kneel at the cross and ask the Lord to forgive my faults. So when the enemy comes to invade my thoughts, I have the presence of mind to tell him, "Shut up, devil. Quit bringing up my past!" There are times when the weight of the world gets heavy on my shoulders, when things ain't going right and I'm contemplating wrong. What a vulnerable state I find myself in that opens the door for that voice once again, reminding me of the past I've vehemently denied. I do consider it, but the thought subsides. At that point, wisdom prevails, and the scheme is brought to light. I recall the fact that I'm engaged in a battle, not physical, but I still have to fight. So I reject the enemy's whisper and respond with a blast, "Shut up, devil. Quit bringing up my past!"

# I Believe

I believe in God and man's ability to transcend, shameful iniquities and the perils of sin. I believe in power relegated to the mind, cognition in motion, the wisdom of our time. I believe in virtue in its purest form, that noble quality that distinguishes from the norm. I believe in love and altruistic sentiment, compassion, thoughtfulness—things often resented. I believe in culture to embrace my kin, and with that same passion, loyalty to a friend. I believe in karma as it relates to justice. The laws of nature have a way to affect us. I believe in me, and with all that I see, I believe that, one day, I'll truly be free.

# The Real G Has Spoken

Have you not heard, have you not read, the genuine oracles of truth? It has been proclaimed throughout the annals of time that the real G would impress it on our hearts and minds. Yet men have chosen their own course in life and determined to know the way. Trends have been strategically set in stone, and without giving thought, we just follow along. Like a soapbox drama, what's right appears wrong—what's popular in culture is glorified in song. Tupac inquired about a heaven for a G, assuming that, in the end, he'd live eternally. But the irony exposed in his demise is that of a brilliant man trapped by lies. "Thug life" expressed the sentiments of his soul, misinterpreted by a culture, exploited by foes. Now the real G has spoken, and only few have heard and ventured even further to examine his word. To search out the purpose and true measure of a man is a noble quest indeed. To inquire of the Lord in the sanctity of his temple will bring you to your knees. But that spells submission and surrender of pride, the humility to admit that we do need a guide. I've heard the voice of the original G, and I'm not talking gangster—I'm talking G-O-D! Do you really wanna know what the G looks like? I challenge you to step into his marvelous light. He'll show you the purpose and plan for your life, if only you'll listen and heed his advice.

# Streets of Sorrow

My heart bled once. Now it pleads for sanity, although I've begged no man's pardon for the tale my life has told. Felt cheated, so I lied. Unconsciously I stole as the layers of misery began to unfold. Took to roaming the countryside and compared my fate to others who were transient and dead while awake. We exchanged foolish wit on religion and politics while drowning our sorrows in the grapes of ferment. Pontificating wildly about the deity of the God-man, I sparked with excitement at the sight of a young lad. He averted his eyes to avoid us as he passed, but I wanted to impress him in a way that would last. So I took the occasion to relive the days before my innocence was stripped away. He listened intently as I drooled through my drawl and concluded with a question that led to a pause. Poised to respond to my inquisitive gist, the young man revealed that he was fatherless. But he didn't mean so in the literal sense, so I urged him to explain. I was astonished by the articulation with which he spoke, demanding my full attention. He shifted his books from right to left, wagged his finger at me, and took a deep breath. "My father became a drifter too. He sold his soul to abandon me. Now that I'm facing life all alone, I'm challenged on every end. I pass these streets nearly every day, knowing that one day will be my last. So whenever I'm confronted by men like yourself, I'm determined to let these streets pass. I pity your plight and the demise of your fate, but I'm headed to school and I can't be late."

# Beautiful People

They're around us all the time, yet we pay them no mind, the beautiful ones who are selfless and kind. The colors of passion reflect in their demeanor. A striking aura of wisdom makes them keener. Most people will agree, and this is no lie. The beautiful spirit is one that'll never die. For they often walk in and out of our lives without the slightest hint of arrogance or foolish pride. I've been graced by the presence of a few. They always seem to know what to say and do. It's as if their intelligence is divinely appointed, but they dare to boast and never flaunt it. The perfect illustration of the Creator in man is the beautiful ones fashioned by his hand.

# She Loves Me 'Cause...

I'm passionately romantic and crazy cool, so in her world, she allows me to rule. Although I'm the king, she's compatible as the queen. We've learned to play the part. I take the lead 'cause I'm intellectually fit and spirituality grounded with humor and wit. Throughout the course of a day, I'll find a clever way to tell her that I love her so. She knows it's true, 'cause that's what I do, even if the mood is melancholy blue. No stressing to leave her guessing if her man is stable. She loves me 'cause she knows her man is able. I provide for her and protect her too, 'cause that's what a man is supposed to do. I acknowledge her as a gift to cherish until the end. She'll never get enough of me, 'cause I'm also her friend.

# The Canvas of Creation

The landscape was laid by a breathless whisper at intervals far beyond what we can conceive. Dimensions, space, and depth of the seas were effortless matters for the Master to achieve. Consider the heavens, how He painted the skies with the complement of a rainbow that annuls our demise. And with one simple stroke of His majestic brush, there was scenery, greenery, animals, and such. Some of these creatures are bound by the waters; others are free to roam. How clever of the Artist to grant them a kingdom distinctively their own. There's a colorful assortment of the lords of the wings. Instinctively they migrate, so freely, it seems. They soar in the day and nest at night; to see them in flight is an awesome sight. But the finishing touches were the grains of dust that formed the essence of man. Ingenious to see the image of the Creator as the Keeper of the land.

# Black Romeo

The chancellor of seduction has his way with women. He's perfected the art of removing their linen. His romantic etiquette to soothe a fetish is a combination of skill and charm. He's well aware and understands the overwhelming desire for a true black man. Black love is strange, like the fruit of the gods. The patron of hearts does know this. So he dares to falter when the chance arises to compliment her sex appeal or cook an unexpected meal. Quality time cannot be ignored for the depths of her mind to be explored. Stimulating her thoughts, body, and soul, urging her forward that she might become whole. And when she's reached her peak and climaxed in stride, Black Romeo remains the complement at her side.

# The Gift and the Giver

Constant is the reminder that God is in control, distributing to the needy, giving rest to the weary soul. Given this assessment, we tend to make our plea as though we are entitled to the fruit from every tree. How often we take for granted the smallest of wonders and deny the source of our strength, until we're faced with tragedy or a fork in the road, a life-changing event. There's a way that seems right that determines our plight and causes us to live only by sight. When deeds are done in the absence of light, our motives are selfish at best. To tap into the source of our power, we discover gifts that are uniquely ours. Your gift may seem a bit different from mine, yet they're all designed to bless humankind. But let us not become too fond of our gifting and what we have inside. When your peers begin to cheer and pat you on the back, the door will open for pride. Standing in the shadow, humbly giving in to the expression of gratitude from within, the reflection of our hearts is on display when we exalt the Giver and acknowledge His way.

# The Psalmist

The legend stands of an extraordinary man who captured the triple crown. He mastered the harp, although it wasn't his art, in the fields his journey began. Over the verdant valleys and pastures where he pastored, to lead the docile sheep, on many a night he chose to compose and forgo the need for sleep. He mastered the art of spiritual war, and the giant came tumbling down. He stood victorious with the enemy's sword over a villain who defied the army of the Lord! He mastered the call of a sovereign King when anointed to reign in his stead. Although he made mistakes that were covered by grace, his accomplishments will never be erased. King David was a man like you and me, with a heart that pleased his God. Rich with rhetoric, a healing balm, he left us a treasure when he penned the psalms.

www.ingramcontent.com/pod-product-compliance
Lightning Source LLC
Chambersburg PA
CBHW071407070526
44578CB00002B/501